Mel Bay Presents

Favorite Carols
for Violin Solo

with Piano Accompaniment

Arranged by John Hollins

1 2 3 4 5 6 7 8 9 0

CONTENTS

INTRODUCTION

Christmas and music have gone "hand in hand" throughout the centuries. Poets and musicians have written some of our best loved and most enduring songs for this season of the year. The easy solos found in this collection can be enjoyed by musicians of all ages. The accompaniments have been kept very basic so that each performance is enhanced.

Have fun — may these selections add to your joyous Christmas season!

O COME, ALL YE FAITHFUL

Note: In each carol, the sign ⸱⸲ represents
the end of each legato phrase

CHORUS

CHORUS

AWAY IN A MANGER

10

ONCE IN ROYAL DAVID'S CITY

Verse 2

SILENT NIGHT

THE FIRST NOWELL

17

CHORUS

CHORUS

marcato

f *rall.*

f *rall.*

18

LITTLE JESUS, SWEETLY SLEEP

THE HOLLY AND THE IVY

Verse 3

Verse 3

CHORUS

CHORUS

à l'écossaise

Ped.

21

WHILE SHEPHERDS WATCHED

22

DING DONG MERRILY ON HIGH!

2nd time *rall.*

24

JOY TO THE WORLD!

O LITTLE TOWN OF BETHLEHEM

28

HARK! THE HERALD ANGELS SING

Solo piano

Verse 1
Solo Verse 2

Verse 1
Verse 2

mp

2nd time al Coda

2nd time al Coda

CODA

CODA

UNTO US A BOY IS BORN

Verse 2

Verse 2

33

Verse 3

WE THREE KINGS

last time to CODA ⊕

last time to CODA ⊕

⊕ CODA

Piano link to 2nd & 3rd time   Dal 𝄋   END

Piano link to 2nd & 3rd time   Dal 𝄋

WHAT CHILD IS THIS?

Piano link to Verse 2

Verse 2

Verse 2 *Cantabile*

IN THE BLEAK MID-WINTER

Verse 3

Verse 3

GOOD KING WENCESLAS

WE WISH YOU A MERRY CHRISTMAS

Brightly and Crisply

Solo

Solo piano

OTHER AVENUE MUSIC PRODUCTS

Solo Books with Keyboard Accompaniment

Favorite Carols for Clarinet Solo
Favorite Carols for Flute Solo
Favorite Carols for Trumpet Solo
Favorite Carols for Violin Solo

Great Classics for Clarinet Solo
Great Classics for Flute Solo
Great Classics for Violin Solo

Distributed exclusively by Mel Bay Publications, Inc.
P.O. Box 66, Pacific, MO 63069
Toll Free 1-800-325-9518